My Dinosaur

Charlotte Raby

OXFORD

UNIVERSITY PRESS

OXFORD
UNIVERSITY PRESS

Great Clarendon Street, Oxford, OX2 6DP, United Kingdom

Oxford University Press is a department of the University
of Oxford. It furthers the University's objective of excellence
in research, scholarship, and education by publishing
worldwide. Oxford is a registered trade mark of Oxford
University Press in the UK and in certain other countries

Text © Charlotte Raby 2016

Illustrations © Daniel Duncan 2016

Inside cover notes written by Becca Heddle

The moral rights of the author have been asserted

First published 2016

British Library Cataloguing in Publication Data
Data available

ISBN: 978-0-19-837100-7

10 9 8 7 6 5 4 3 2

Paper used in the production of this book is a natural,
recyclable product made from wood grown in sustainable forests.
The manufacturing process conforms to the environmental
regulations of the country of origin.

Printed in China by Golden Cup

Acknowledgements

Series Editor: Nikki Gamble

The publisher would like to thank the following for permission to
reproduce photographs:
Cover&back cover: Shutterstock; **fct&p7**: Dr Manuel Suárez/
Universidad Andrés Bello; **fcb&p16tm**: Richard Green/
Alamy Stock Photo; **p1**: Shutterstock; **p4**: Sebastian Silva/EFE;
p5&10: reprinted by permission from Macmillan Publishers
Ltd/doi:10.1038 /nature14307/copyright2015; **p8,9,11&16tl**:
Dr Manuel Suárez/Universidad Andrés Bello; **p12,14&15**: Gabriel
Lio; **p13**: Eitan Abramovich/Getty Images; **p16bl**: Shutterstock;
p16bm: Jason Edwards/Getty Images.

Contents

Meet Diego

I am Diego.
I come from Chile.

Me!

Chile

4

When I was seven, I dug up some **fossils**. They were from a **dinosaur**!

What is a Fossil?

Fossils are animals and plants that turn into rocks.

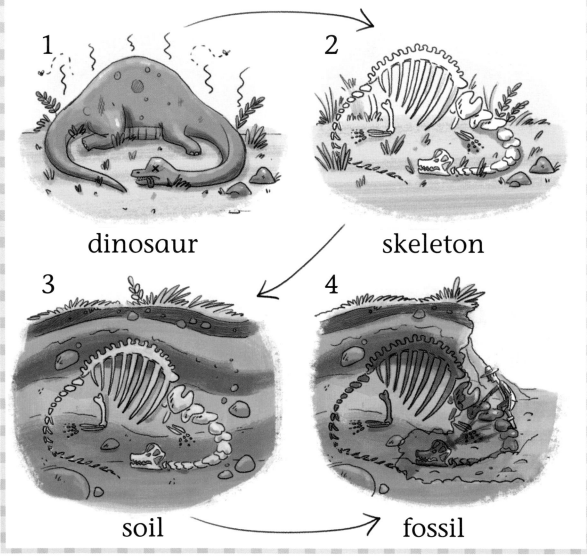

1 dinosaur

2 skeleton

3 soil

4 fossil

I didn't think my fossils were important. But they were!

Me with the fossils when I was seven!

Fossil Hunting

We were **camping** at Black Hill.

Me and Dad

Dad was looking at rocks for his job.

pick

book

brush

But I was fossil hunting!

The Dinosaur Dig

I hit a chunk of soil. The soil had some objects in it.

Fossils

I got Mum and Dad. They got help.

Soon, there were lots of adults digging.

The dinosaur dig

Diego's Dinosaur

Diego dug up a dinosaur!
It was not like a **T. rex**.
It fed on plants.

Diego's dinosaur is a Chilesaurus.

"No one had seen this sort of dinosaur until we dug up the fossils," said Diego.

T. rex and Chilesaurus

This is a T. rex.

big skull

sharp teeth

short neck

short arms

long tail

It fed on animals.

This is a Chilesaurus.

little skull

smooth teeth

long tail

long neck

short arms

It fed on plants.

My dinosaur!

15

Glossary

camping

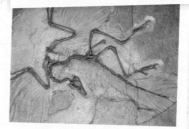

Chilesaurus

dinosaur

fossils

T. rex

Index